WWII SPITFIRE PILOT
At the Battle of Britain

F.J. Beerling

Illustrated by Gareth Bowler

| Sqn Ldr
Alfred "Alfie" Rattington-Smythe | Flt Lt
Fletchibald "Fletch" Ratbottom | Sgt
Colin "Cannon Fodder" Roach |

ISBN: 9780993384240

Published by Fairyfaye Publications
For events and all enquiries email fairyfayepublications@gmail.com

Edited by Denise Smith www.dspublishingservices.co.uk

Special thanks to:
David Brocklehurst MBE, Kent Battle of Britain Museum, Hawkinge,
for the verification of the historical content of this book.
Poetic licence has been applied on occasions.

Fairyfaye
Publications
www.fairyfayepublications.co.uk

Book design by Gareth Bowler

Printed in Great Britain

For "The Few" and everyone who fought for us in
the Battle of Britain.

F.B

For every brave RAF pilot, past, present and future.

G.B

Special thanks to Julian Jennings without whom this book
would not have been possible.

To Mark and Megan, the right way up...

J.J

*O*nce upon a long ago, back in 1933,
Hitler became the leader of a country called Germany.

He then attacked Poland; seizing land and weapons galore,
And this took place in 1939; so Britain went to war.

*A*nnounced by Neville Chamberlain, Prime Minister at the time,
His speech was aired across the airwaves, on September 3rd, 1939.

*S*irens went off; lights went out and people fled underground,
To shelter from the hail of bullets, and bombs dropping all around.

Food was rationed; clothes recycled and identity tags were worn,
But Britain still refused to surrender; so battle lines were drawn.

And for six long years the war it raged;
Life got very tough,
Until Germany surrendered in 1945;
They'd finally had enough...

... *T*hey had enough of being attacked, as into our skies they flew,
Trying to wipe out the Royal Air Force; at the beginning of WWII.

But we had to attack and fire back, on July the 10th 1940.
When Hitler's planes started bombing us;
That man was mean and naughty.

He blew up airfields and our ships to stop us winning the war,
Then planned to cross the sea by boat;
landing soldiers upon our shore.

And so, the Battle of Britain began; with Messerschmitts flying over,

And dog fights with Hurricanes and our Spitfires;
Blazed above the cliffs of Dover.

As pilots sat around
Playing cards;
Drinking tea
And scoffing buns,

Waiting for that
Call to scramble,
The mechanics
Readied their guns.

So with a hip flask and a compass and gloves that fitted tight;
A parachute in case they bailed, and some goggles for the flight.

And from his flying suit down to his boots, our pilot was prepared,
To blast the Germans out of the sky; no enemy plane was spared.

Into the cockpit they scrambled and then it was, "CHOCKS AWAY!"
As they flew themselves high into battle, hoping to save the day.

*B*ehind their armoured windscreen,
with loaded guns on either side,
Instructions via the radio headset, and boiled sweeties for the ride!

Off they flew into the air, day after day and night after night,
Never knowing where they were going or if this was their final flight.

They flew their planes, shot the baddies
And steered with rudder pedals,
Whilst flying their squadrons into battle, some got bravery medals!

*B*ack on the ground, the air-raid sound
Sent panic through their hearts,
As women in warehouses downed their tools;
They were making aeroplane parts.

...**A**nd then, later on, they drove our tanks, as well as flying planes;
As if that wasn't impressive enough, they even operated trains!

15

Pots and pans were melted down;
When planes were running low,
And they recycled metal railings!
Bet that's something you didn't know.

Britain was one giant airfield. The Americans and Polish helped out,
Wooing our ladies with their swanky accents...
...And driving trucks about.

*T*he Yanks chewed gum and so did our kids,
We even made planes from old dustbin lids!

*F*our months later and the battle was over,
No more dog fights across the cliffs of Dover.

We were shot at; blown up;
Bombed and blitzed,
Running out of pots and pans
And London was in bits!

Although the war was far from over;
In fact it had just begun,
We celebrated this massive victory
With a cup of tea and a bun!

Yes, we had won
The Battle of Britain
It ended on Halloween.

Oh, did I mention that
Driving a truck...?

...*W*as, in fact, our very own Queen!

Faye Beerling grew up in a children's home, which was full of children and not a lot of toys. To amuse herself Faye developed a big imagination and was always being told off for making up stories! Faye also loves history and decided to combine the two. The results are entertaining!

Gareth Bowler didn't grow up and drew this book. He went to Art College somewhere in the past and failed. After several uneventful years drawing bears, Gareth now specialises in rat and cockroach illustration (and the occasional aeroplane and, now, by the looks of it, trucks!).